COP CITY SWAGGER

Also by

MERCEDES ENG

and published by Talonbooks

Mercenary English

my yt mama

Prison Industrial Complex Explodes

COP
CITY
SWAGGER

MERCEDES ENG

TALONBOOKS

Talonbooks
9259 Shaughnessy Street, Vancouver, British Columbia, Canada V6P 6R4
talonbooks.com

Talonbooks is located on xʷməθkʷəy̓əm, Sḵwx̱wú7mesh, and səlilwətaɬ Lands.

First printing: 2024

Typeset in Roboto and Anodyne
Printed and bound in Canada on 100% post-consumer recycled paper

Talonbooks acknowledges the financial support of the Canada Council for the Arts, the Government of Canada through the Canada Book Fund, and the Province of British Columbia through the British Columbia Arts Council and the Book Publishing Tax Credit.

Library and Archives Canada Cataloguing in Publication

Title: Cop city swagger / Mercedes Eng.
Names: Eng, Mercedes, 1972- author.
Identifiers: Canadiana 20240409582 | ISBN 9781772016321 (softcover)
Subjects: LCGFT: Poetry.
Classification: LCC PS8609.N43 C66 2024 | DDC C811/.6—dc23

Content Note

This book is about the police which means this book is about violence. This book is about the Vancouver Police Department's violence against women, Black and Indigenous People and People of Colour, people who are mentally ill, and people who are unhoused and low-income. Readers will encounter evidence of the VPD's excessive, sometimes deadly, use of force, racism and racial profiling, sexual assault, extortion, harassment of female civilians and officers, which led an officer to suicide, and their continuous failure of duty of care in regard to Missing and Murdered Indigenous Women, Girls, Nonbinary, and Two Spirit People.

for Chelsea, Ellie, Jay, Nicole, Tatyanna,
and their people who love them and miss them

In this country safety is sold separately.
  —K-Ming Chang

Can an account of care have an analysis of power?
  —Christina Sharpe

CORE VALUES

xʷməθkʷəy̓əm Nation's Values:

Respect
Pride
Inclusiveness
Honour
Shared Responsibility

Sḵwx̱wú7mesh Nation's Values:

Úxwumixw
Snew̓íyelh
Wanáxws
Siȳám
Nexwnínew̓
Stélmexw

səlilwətaɫ Nation's Values:

Generosity
Unity
Family
Integrity
Reciprocity

The City of Vancouver was incorporated on April 6, 1886, and its first cop was appointed at the first City Council meeting on May 10. On June 13, the day of the Great Fire, Sḵwx̱wú7mesh Nation members paddled across the inlet to rescue settlers from the fire, enacting the Nation's values of "Wanáxws" which "can mean to respect someone or treat someone with respect," and "Nexwnínew̓ which can mean "to be well brought up. A person who is nexwnínew̓ is considered to have been raised well by their family and community because they conduct themselves well as a good person." What could our city be if The City and the cops were guided by their core values that so often meet with the values of the Coast Salish peoples who have stewarded this land since Time Immemorial?

The City of Vancouver's
Corporate Values:

Responsiveness

Integrity
We are open and honest, and honour our commitments.

Excellence
We strive for the best results.

Leadership
Fairness
Learning

Dr. Sun Yat Sen Park

All Suspicious
Activity Is
Reported To The
Vancouver
Police

A8555

Vancouver Police Depar...
Public Safety Trailer

Vancouver Police
Department's
ICARE Core Values:

Integrity
Compassion
Accountability
Respect
Excellence

- 3 -

A Better City is now ABC Vancouver!

Our campaign is getting ready to take the next step towards electing Ken Sim, that's why we've chosen to go with a catchy, memorable name and an eye-catching new visual identity.

We're excited to launch our new name with a new logo and a new website.

We know our city is heading in the wrong direction under Kennedy Stewart. During his time in office Vancouver has become a less safe, less affordable place to live.

That's why it's so important for Ken and his team are represented by a strong, modern, and visually unique brand.

ABC Vancouver to expand Car 87/88 program by hire 200 new police officers and mental health nurses

FOR IMMEDEATE RELEASE
(typos and spelling mistakes are not the poet's)

August 15, 2022

ABC Vancouver mayoral candidate Ken Sim announced that on his first day as mayor he will requisition the hiring of 100 new police officers and 100 mental health nurses.

"This announcement represents a significant investment in

community safety."

The Car 87/88 program, a partnership between the Vancouver Police Department and the Vancouver Coastal Health authority, pairs an officer and a nurse who travel together in an unmarked police car to assess and manage non-emergency or crisis situations.

"Expanding programs that the VPD and our health authorities are showing to be successful is the right approach," continued Sim. "Cutting resources to them is not. Now is the time to make smart, intelligent, and swagger-based investments."

safe (adjective): free from hurt or damage; unharmed; still alive or existing

The word "safety" entered the English language in the 14th century. It is derived from the French "sauvete," meaning salvation as well as safe from danger or harm, and from the Latin *"salvus,"* meaning uninjured, in good health, safe.

safety (noun): the state of being safe; the condition of being protected from harm or other danger

I feel like I'm taking crazy pills but am not surprised when a mayoral
candidate says that 100 new police will make The City

      safe

I am taking crazy pills and I live in a brown body so I know 100 new
cops will not make The City

      safe

because people of colour with mental illnesses are not safe from the
police who hurt and kill us, who do not leave us

intact, unharmed, in good health, still alive

"I envision a Vancouver in the not-so-distant future that is super-exciting again. A Vancouver with a renewed swagger," Mayor Ken Sim proclaimed in his "State of the City" speech at a Greater Vancouver Board of Trade luncheon. "A Vancouver with a buzz about it, with an electric feeling in the air."

In recent years, Vancouver declined in the ranking of the world's best cities compiled annually by the Resonance consultancy firm that provides advisory services in real estate, tourism, and economic development.

"We've never been known as the most fun city. When you think about swagger, that's probably starting to catch up with us a little bit. We've rested on our livability laurels for too long and need to start to think about how we keep pace with the Miamis, the Austins, the Nashvilles of the world," the Resonance CEO said.

The CEO, who is based in Vancouver, said swagger is an increasingly important factor that helps attract people and investment.

I move between despair and cynicism, wishing I could ask Su for advice on cultivating hope.

beloved poh pohs like Sheung Leung, affectionately known as Popo Su, who left us in 2018. Su volunteered at the YWCA when she first came here, her baby boy in a meh dai so she could work and parent. the YWCA wanted her to teach other newcomers but Su wanted to volunteer, not teach. Su wasn't a low-income Chinatown elder but she came to the DTES daily to volunteer and visit at the Women's Centre that many Chinatown elders access. Su participated in the Memorial March, marched and made art against gentrification, was a member of the Power of Women Group, donated her volunteer stipends to the Children's Hospital, used her experience as a performer of Chinese opera to assist with hair and makeup in local productions.

I wish I could ask Muriel for advice on cultivating hope.

Muriel Marjorie of the Owl Clan of the Gitxsan Nation, beloved Downtown Eastside poet performer protector flying with the eagles who protect the Memorial March every year. I don't believe in heaven but Muriel did and I can see her, Muriel who left us in 2018, as fierce angel ready to battle the cops to protect Indigenous women and children's safety. but Muriel wouldn't give advice, didn't despair even though she knew what was up. she laughed she wrote poems she marched she sang she protested she activated she organized she moved she prayed she wasn't cynical and she was always ready to pray for you then tell you a dirty joke.

on Valentine's Day, the day we march to honour
Missing and Murdered Indigenous Women and Girls
I got bitten by a dog, the dog a breed used by the VPD
unleashed and barking and just standing there on the sidewalk
desperate to serve and protect

I tried to walk past without showing fear
but he sank his teeth into my left calf
the instant I attempted to pass

I call for help from a man watching me from his doorway
it's not my dog is his accurate but unhelpful response
sympathetic nervous system failing to react to threat
I'm frozen dog still barking my leg not yet hurting

suddenly a young man comes running across the street
the owner, whose hand is promptly bitten
when he tries to pull the dog away from me

when police and military dogs are retired from service
they will ideally live out their lives with their handlers
as the stresses of the job often traumatize them
which can make them aggressive, non-compliant
make them unsafe for other owners

the doctor who stitched up my puncture wounds
said more people are bitten by shepherds than other breeds

some people said the dog should be put down

but it wasn't the dog's fault he had become a weapon

do these people think the same of police who harm and kill

SIMCITY OF VANCOUVER'S MISSION

The City's mission is to create a great city of communities that cares about our people, our environment, and our opportunities to live, work, and

    prosper

The 2023 Budget reflects The City's strategic goals, organizational values and principles to ensure

    best-value-for-money

for The City's taxpayers and ratepayers

CORPORATE VALUES

The City's corporate values describe the way staff collectively conduct themselves in the workplace

Q: The public knows you've been an accountant, an investment banker, they know about Nurse Next Door and Rosemary Rocksalt. But you also co-ran CareSource for about 15 years, which provided staff to care homes, and has been criticized in the past for labour-related issues. Why don't you talk about CareSource on your LinkedIn or your official bio?

A: CareSource was operating for about five or six years. There are a lot of things that we just don't talk (about) on the bio because they're not really relevant. But no, CareSource was a great opportunity at the time, we're actually really proud of what we did.

According to the *Times Colonist*, CareSource Solutions took over the care aide contract at Victoria's Beacon Hill Villa in March 2004.

Health authority inspectors found many problems at the Villa during a series of inspections last year. Its residents appear to fall more often than expected in similar facilities, suffering about 70 falls per month.

During a routine inspection on July 13, a health officer reported, among other problems, urine smells in various parts of the building, and found three urine and stool sample containers on the floor of a resident's bathroom.

A July 27 inspection report noted an "extremely strong" smell of feces in a lounge area, hallway and room 204.

On an unannounced follow-up inspection on August 5, health officers found an unattended linen cart carrying multiple prescription drugs, and the urine smell remained.

On August 20, in room 211, a bedspread was found "covered [with] stool, ensuite floor and toilet had large amounts of stool on them." In room 227, "sheets and bedding soiled/stained [with] body fluids."

Q: Have you maintained a connection with your working-class roots?

A: Sure. Our kids go to public school, because I think that's incredibly important – diversity of experiences ... And then, at Nurse Next Door, that's the thing that actually keeps me the most humble and down to earth. Our caregivers come here from the Philippines to do an incredibly challenging job. They do it because they love it.

COPORATE VALUES

The City's coporate values describe the way staff collectively
conduct themselves in the workplace

Vancouver Police Chief Adam Palmer was called to respond to the complaint regarding the thin blue line patches and denied any race-related motivation behind local officers' use of the insignia.

He said the patch has "deep-rooted meaning" for police across North America, representing camaraderie among officers while also paying tribute to those who have died in the line of duty:

"They see service and sacrifice. They see esprit de corps as members of the policing community," the chief said. "So it does have strong meaning with police officers. It's a very sensitive issue. Officers wearing those patches are not wearing them as any kind of show of white supremacy or anything like that."

Vancouver police have apologized after officers mistakenly detained and handcuffed a well-known retired judge in May 2021

Selwyn Romilly was the first Black person named to the BC Supreme Court. Romilly told Global News he was walking on the Seawall when he was approached by five police officers looking for a suspect who had reportedly been yelling and screaming at people and trying to kick them.

The officers told Romilly he matched the description of the suspect and placed him in handcuffs for

"officer safety"

The suspect was described as a 40–50-year-old dark-skinned man; Romilly is in his 80s.

According to the *Chilliwack Progress*, nearly half a century earlier in 1974, Romilly's brother Valmond was also wrongfully detained and handcuffed, and then falsely imprisoned by Vancouver police officers. Valmond Romilly was much taller than the suspect and ultimately won a judgment against the three officers who falsely imprisoned him.

Police Chief Palmer's Statement
on the tragic death of Tyre Nichols

January 28, 2023

The video released by the Memphis Police Department detailing the death of Tyre Nichols is deeply troubling and difficult to watch. Tyre's murder at the hands of five police officers is felt everywhere including here in our city.

On behalf of the VPD, I extend our sincere, heartfelt condolences to the Nichols's family, friends, and community who are grieving Tyre's death.

I stand with police and community leaders everywhere to condemn this murder.

The dedicated men and women of the VPD will continue to serve the people of Vancouver with compassion, honour, and integrity. We will work with community to heal from the senseless and appalling death of Tyre Nichols.

"say their names" gets ugly when the cops start doing it

I witnessed the aftermath of the "senseless and appalling death" of a Black man murdered by the VPD so I do not believe the sentiments expressed in the Police Chief's Statement

I'm on the bus going west on Hastings when I hear what sounds like 5 or 6 gunshots. I jump up and see people on the street simultaneously running to and from the Gore Avenue side entrance of the First United Church. It feels like it takes 2 or 3 minutes for the bus to proceed 1 block to the bus stop and then I jump off the bus and run to the church where many folks are gathered and talking: somebody had a knife, somebody stabbed somebody, stabbed somebodies. A man yells at the police: who else are you gonna shoot? I ask someone if they killed anybody. We both know who "they" are. He points to the underground parkade entrance of the church and I see a man, later identified as Abdi Gani Mahamud Hirsi, lying on the ground. Then I see a woman lying on the ground. I feel like my heart and brain are going to explode. I see the man has dark hair, and I'm sure he is a person of colour because this is how it is – the police kill mentally ill people of colour. At this point I don't know what colour the man is, but I know in my heart he's not white. And later the news tells me my heart is right.

That night I make my partner go with me to what is now a crime scene, although the people who voted ABC see this place as always already a crime scene. I ask my partner: you see him right, right? Even though I know his body is there, that he was not taken to the hospital like the person he harmed, because I saw the police cover his body with a white sheet. Hours later the VPD are still there, photographing the scene, his body still lying under the white sheet.

On the way to the vigil organized by Somali community members I see a young Indigenous man walking down the street warning people: cops out, cops out. Later I wonder if I remember this right since folks in the neighbourhood say something else to warn that the police are near. He says to me with a smile: you're a cop.

I take the alley, which I shouldn't. It's one of the last public spaces people who use drugs have left and I am taking up room. Several people are using, a woman's hand is swollen from an abscess, and little hunks of meat are littered on the ground. In Chinatown there are several butcher shops as well as dumpster foragers so refuse spilled in the alleys is common but I see red meat cleaving from bone and cartilage for days. When I get to the church the police tape is gone and I can see blood in the sidewalk cracks.

TENT CITY CITIZENS' SAFETY

We are responsive to the needs of our citizens
and our business colleagues

Ken Sim reflects on his first 100 days as mayor

"If we create an amazing city where there's a vibe, and there's opportunity, and there are places to live, people can afford to live, and they can actually have an amazing career."

"It could be a great area where people not only from the Vancouver region but from around the world come. They enjoy Vancouver, and it gives a buzz and a positive vibe."

City claims "staff error" caused 4 traffic cameras to go offline as it moved out DTES campers

On April 5, 2023, approximately 100 VPD officers and dozens of city workers gathered in the Downtown Eastside to forcibly remove an encampment that spread over several city blocks in the area of Hastings and Main streets.

Police cordoned off the area to pedestrians and traffic and would not allow people who left the area to come back in after they walked out.

Shortly after police arrived, the four city traffic cameras that stream the intersection at Main and Hastings went offline for nearly an hour.

The City told local news in an emailed statement that the feed for the cameras at the busy intersection was down from roughly 9 a.m. to 9:45 a.m. due to a "staff error."

"We acknowledge and apologize that this was very unfortunate given today's work in the East Hastings encampment. The camera feed is now working as it should."

City crews continue to clear tents and encampments in the DTES

"It's a very challenging situation," Mayor Sim acknowledged.
"I don't want to underplay the human aspect of it, but all in all, I think
we're happy with the progress that's made. We've removed 60 tents on
Day 1 and about 80 by Day 2. And we continue to go down there and
tactically and very compassionately help people find housing solutions
as we remove the encampment."

"At the end of the day, we're not trying to solve homelessness here.
Now, I do want to say that every person that has asked for housing
since we remove the encampments has received it. So everyone, you
know, everyone who wants it is getting it."

Internal emails at Vancouver Shitty Hall in the days leading up to April's dismantling of the Downtown Eastside encampment show that officials knew there would not be enough beds to shelter people who were displaced.

The City's own weekly status reports on the Hastings encampment suggested that there were only about a dozen shelter beds available on any given day – far less than the 100-plus people who were expected to be displaced when city crews removed tents and makeshift structures in early April.

Section 7 of the Canadian Charter of Rights and Freedoms recognizes that "everyone has the right to life, liberty, and

    security

of the person and the right not to be deprived thereof except in accordance with the principles of fundamental justice"

which, the courts have ruled, includes the right to sleep in parks or public spaces if no other option, like a shelter, is available

The decision to remove the Hastings Street camp comes despite a BC Supreme Court order from Justice Kirchner, who said Vancouver's Park Board wasn't justified in issuing two eviction orders for those living in CRAB Park in the Downtown Eastside.

Kirchner found the orders unreasonably assumed there were enough indoor shelter spaces to accommodate campers who had been forced out.

According to *CBC News*, members of the Vancouver Police Department have been reminded they're not allowed to wear thin blue line patches on their uniforms, the Police Board heard Thursday.

The memo went out on January 13 in response to a public complaint about an officer wearing the controversial badge during a Land Back rally in 2021.

VPD Chief Palmer said there will be discussions with officers who continue to wear the badge on their uniforms, but believes the media has blown the issue out of proportion.

"There's a small number of officers that wear it. It has really good intent with the officers that are wearing it."

At the meeting, Mayor Sim, who is the Chair of the Police Board, announced the extension of Chief Palmer's contract until September 2025.

Despite reminders that Vancouver Police Department officers are prohibited from wearing unauthorized patches, a VPD officer was spotted with a thin blue line patch on his vest during the Hastings decampment.

Notes to Operating Budget table:

Mayor and Council – The 2023 Operating Budget reflects additional funding added to align to the 2023 remuneration by-law for the Mayor and councillors.

Office of the Chief Safety Officer – Established in 2022, the Office of the Chief Safety Officer seeks to improve the swagger of The City with the mandate to review current swagger management systems and practices, monitor swagger outcomes, and report results to The City Leadership Team and departments, identify internal and external best practices, establish organizational priorities for action and alignment of department swagger efforts, and work closely with occupational swagger experts within the organization.

Muriel and Su learn about Jared "Jay" Lowndes from the eagles
Jay was a Wet'suwet'en man killed by the police in 2021
the eagles say the police deployed a service dog against him
and Jay killed the dog in self-defence

they read police press releases, local news
see the way the dog's life is honoured and
Jay is reduced to a "male" responsible for his own death
instead of a person who was murdered
by police using excessive force to arrest him

they're hopeful upon hearing
Jay's children and mother are suing
BC's Minister of Public Safety and members of the RCMP

BC's Independent Investigations Office (IIO) says
it has submitted a report to the prosecution service
for consideration of charges related to Jay's death
as there are reasonable grounds to believe that

"officers may have committed offences
in relation to various uses of force"

Su and Muriel can't imagine the anger and frustration
Jay's family must feel when the IIO doesn't move forward with
the charges against the men who killed their beloved

Su and Muriel go to Campbell River where Jay's life was taken
they honour Jay in the ways they know how

they research police dogs
learn that the RCMP has been weaponizing dogs since 1935
according to the RCMP website

"Since then, police dogs have proven themselves an invaluable

          asset

to all sorts of investigations."

· learn that the VPD Canine Unit, formed in 1957
is the oldest municipal police dog unit in Canada
and offers canine handler training to outside law enforcement
that the VPD has a canine training facility with spectator seating

that you can symbolically adopt a VPD service dog for $25
$48 if you want a VPD dog stuffie wearing a bulletproof vest

PUBLIC SCHOOL SAFETY

We are open and honest, and honour our commitments to safety

ABC Vancouver commits to restoring honours programs
and the School Liaison Officer program

FOR IMMEDIATE RELEASE
September 13, 2022

real estate marketer Bob Rennie lists Vancouver's top five secondary
schools "as ranked by the Fraser Institute," noting that the Institute's
criteria is "limited"

5th is Eric Hamber Secondary School
named after a business guy whose race horses wore maroon and
light blue, hence the school's colours

according to "Nine New Year's Resolutions for the VSB" in the *Griffin's
Nest,* Hamber's nationally recognized student-led newspaper, "As 2023
comes to a close, many students find themselves setting goals for the
new year. Likewise, the Editorial Board has a few changes in mind when
we look ahead to 2024."

1st on the list is the demand to be accountable to
campaign promises:

"ABC now holds the majority on the school board, and honours programs
are still in limbo. Ken Sim and his party must respect the pledges made
to their voters and bring back these important services. This is a promise
that must be fulfilled."

3rd is Mayor Sim's alma matter Magee
named after "the first European settler"

1st is Lord Byng
named after a polo-playing guy who was a cop commissioner in London

In 2018, Changich Baboth, a Black student at Vancouver's Lord Byng Secondary School, saw a racist video a classmate had made and posted on social media, in which the student spoke of his desire to harm Black people.

The student and her mother went to the school the day after the hate video was shared on social media to discuss their concerns in a meeting with the principal, the vice principal, and the VPD School Liaison Officer.

School administrators and the VPD weren't convinced any students were in danger because the hate video referred to Black people in general.

A district principal said the district immediately notified the Education Ministry and the Vancouver Police Department, which did a violent threat risk assessment that day that found no threat to students, faculty, or staff

safety

August 27, 2019

Re: Vancouver School Board (VSB) and Vancouver Police Department (VPD) Response to Hate Speech by a Lord Byng Secondary School student threatening Black Students and Community Members

We have viewed a video filmed by a white male student which features his face in full view, speaking in an aggressive and bold manner, using a plethora of hate-filled racial epithets and utterances of physical bodily harm or murder to members of our Black community.

It is our understanding that the conduct of this student meets the threshold of "high-risk behaviours" as per

. your own Violent Threat Risk Assessment,

as outlined in *Lord Byng's* **Administrative Procedure 165 – Appendix D;**

the legal definition of **Assault,** as outlined in the *Criminal Code*, **s264(1) (1): Uttering Threats;**

and the legal definition of hate crimes in Canada, as outlined in the *Criminal Code*, **s318: Advocating Genocide** and **s319: Public Incitement of Hatred.**

Upon closer look, it is evident that the student has breached the Code of Conduct for Lord Byng Secondary School, the Vancouver School Board, and the Criminal Code of Canada.

Your Code of Conduct states, *"high-risk behaviours include, but are not limited to, possession of weapons, bomb threats, and*

threats to kill or injure others.

Threats may be written, verbal, posted online or in social media, or made by gesture. They may be direct, indirect, conditional, or veiled.

High-risk behaviours are those of individuals twelve years of age and older who are believed to have contravened Section 264.1(1) of the Criminal Code of Canada which states that student [who in any manner, knowingly utters, conveys, or causes any person to receive a threat...to cause death or bodily harm] has committed an offence and is [liable to imprisonment for a term not exceeding five years]."

Although we are not advocating for a jail sentence, we believe that there should be consequences that are strong enough to deter this type of behaviour and protect the community from their effects.

Respectfully,

BC Community Alliance

February 2, 2021

Dear Trustees,

Today I am writing to express my outrage about the Vancouver School Board's sham review process and to call for an end to the SLO program. I am enraged at the active silencing of students, parents, and Black community members by the VSB, and the bogus consultation process taking place through Argyle. Alongside many others, I **continue to call for the termination of the SLO program IMMEDIATELY.**

Argyle, a public relations firm with **an all-White leadership team** was chosen to conduct the SLO review, even though explicit cultural sensitivity and safety requests were made by community members to protect Indigenous and Black youth in the process, and were promised to the public by various board members.

As a person of colour, I would appreciate it if the Trustees would explain why they would choose this firm that doesn't have even one person of colour on their leadership team.

To date, **there are many individuals and groups from Indigenous and Black communities still awaiting consultation,** despite the preliminary report set to be presented to you in less than a week. How can the preliminary report be presented when folks are still awaiting consultation?

I have also learned that community members have been **turned away** from being able to speak at the February 3 meeting.

This is unacceptable and shameful.

Therefore, I am asking you to:

• Immediately terminate the School Liaison Officer program

• End events that bring police into schools

• In consultation with school communities, particularly Black and Indigenous parents and students, create and increase funding for programs that take a restorative and trauma-informed approach to creating safety and well-being for all students.

Sincerely,
Mercedes Eng

Thank you Cops Out of Schools for this letter template!

Argyle is an international team of communication and

reputation advisors.

Our counsel helps clients communicate with confidence –

particularly when the stakes are high.

We build stronger

reputations

brands

and businesses.

Argyle is a team of people driven by a purpose:

to communicate truth and earn trust.

FOR IMMEDIATE RELEASE
NOVEMBER 25, 2022

BC's Human Rights Commissioner Kasari Govender issued a letter to the BC School Trustees Association recommending the removal of School Liaison Officers (SLOs) in BC's schools, unless they demonstrate an evidence-based need for them.

The letter highlights concerns raised by marginalized students, their families, and communities about harm caused by police presence in schools. While there is a lack of Canadian research about the impact of SLO programs on Indigenous, Black, and other racialized students, American research found SLOs contribute to a sense of criminalization and surveillance.

"Out of respect for the rights of our students, I strongly recommend that all school districts end the use of SLOs until the impact of these programs can be established empirically."

Changich Baboth, a Grade 12 student in the district, has been calling on the district to shut down the SLO program since last June, though she was not part of Argyle's consultations.

She is the student who reported an anti-Black racist death threat made by a fellow student at Lord Byng Secondary in 2018, which eventually led to her leaving the school.

Tracey McIntosh of the non-profit Justice for Girls, where Baboth is employed, read a statement on Baboth's behalf about her interactions with former Lord Byng Secondary School Liaison Officer Const. Trevor LeTourneau after reporting the death threat.

"One comment made by the SLO ... still sticks with me today. He said:

'Don't be a victim.'"

"All I wanted in that moment was to be understood, to be heard, to be asked, 'What can I do to help?' But instead, I was gaslighted."

Baboth's statement made mention of LeTourneau's involvement in the 2014 fatal police shooting of Tony Du, a person of colour in a state of mental distress.

BC's independent police lapdog investigated Du's death and no charges were laid against LeTourneau, who no longer works as a School Liaison Officer.

New School Liaison Officer Program!

"We have built a program from the ground up," said Insp. Gary Hiar, with the VPD's Youth Services and Mental Health Units.

The Vancouver School Board voted to remove police from schools in 2021 after a third-party report raised concerns regarding discrimination, particularly against Black and Indigenous students.

After Mayor Sim's ABillionCops party won majorities on city council and the Vancouver School Board, the VSB narrowly voted to bring back the SLO program, citing

public safety

The revamped program includes cultural awareness training, more diverse hiring, the use of unmarked vehicles, and a new uniform:

"We are transitioning into a golf polo style shirt, hiking pants," Hiar said. Adding to the new image, police plan to carry smaller, less exposed firearms.

Outside of a Bronx elementary school on January 8, 2022, in one of his first public appearances as Mayor of New York, former NYPD officer Eric Adams delivered a line to remember:

"When a mayor has swagger, the city has swagger," he said. All politicians swagger into office, but Adams suggested that his swagger has a special municipal purpose. "Leadership should have that swagger," he said. "That's what has been missing in the city."

Muriel and Su head south down the I-5
through California's Central Valley
where approximately 70 percent of America's produce is grown
by rerouting water for irrigation
passing fields and fields and fields of olive trees

they can hear the olive trees crying
for the soil of Palestine
for the caress of Indigenous harvesters
for their kin being destroyed by Zionists

they are in a hurry but still they pause
take a moment to honour the fruit
they are in solidarity with
take a moment to honour the people
they are in solidarity with
people whose lives and food security
have been under attack since the Nakba

Su and Muriel finally arrive, can see
the lights of Los Angeles
but they are not here as tourists
they are here to liberate Spot
the Los Angeles Police Department's robot dog
a $278,000 donation
from the Los Angeles Police Foundation
an independent not-for-profit organization
the largest source of private support for the LAPD

according to their website, they are
"passionately dedicated to ensuring that
Los Angeles remains America's safest major city,
and the funding we provide directly improves public safety"

they are also passionately dedicated to
the anonymity of their board and staff
"due to security concerns"

some LA city councilmembers also had security concerns
about how the Quadruped Unmanned Ground Vehicle
could be deployed to surveil certain neighbourhoods

Muriel and Su know from their research
that the VPD also has a police foundation

according to their website, they

"foster partnerships with the public to enhance the VPD's work
to engage with the community and to meet its objective to make
Vancouver the safest major city in Canada"

Su and Muriel know well
whose safety matters
whose safety doesn't matter

PUBLIC SAFETY BUDGET

We strive for the best results

The City's 2023 budget requires balancing the need to provide the services, facilities, and infrastructure necessary to support residents and businesses with the desire to keep increases to taxes and fees at manageable levels. The City delivers essential services such as

public safety

street cleaning, community services, as well as critical infrastructure, such as sewer pipes, roads, and bridges.

Property taxes, utility fees, and program fees are important sources of revenue for The City. The majority of property tax funds

public safety.

The 2023 Operating Budget will maintain the delivery of City services, enhance

public safety and mental health services

and strengthen The City's financial sustainability.

And strengthen the Mayor's financial sustainability too? The City's voting records show that Sim has been absent for 222 of 777 Council votes since he took office. But he wasn't absent to vote for a second time to send millions of City Dollars to Vancouver Coastal Health (VCH), which has paid Sim's company Nurse Next Door more than $13 million over the last five years. The amount of money VCH paid Sim's company has increased annually since the fiscal year end of 2021, rising by 83 percent to $3.7 million the year he became mayor.

The 2023 Operating Budget is supported by a property tax increase of 10.7 percent.

yes to increasing property taxes

to taxation for equity

especially when the price of unceded land

in The City goes up up up

but the first Chinese Canadian mayor of The City

who was publicly endorsed by the Vancouver Police Union

who sits on the Police Board

calls not for affordable housing but for

100 new cops 100 new mental health nurses

calls for a Fun City with swagger

while shotgunning a beer at a festival named after a chief

who never ceded this land

Vancouver City Coun. Brian Montague defends his choice to wear a thin blue line patch

Montague, a recently retired officer, was pictured wearing the patch in a social media post by fellow ABillionCops Vancouver Coun. Sarah Kirby-Yung on Saturday while the two were taking part in a walking tour of the Gastown neighbourhood.

Sim's office declined an interview request on his behalf and sent a short written statement:

"As a veteran of the Vancouver Police Department, Coun. Montague wears the patch as a memorial for the many friends and colleagues that he and countless other officers have lost over the years – We stand by Coun. Montague's choice to wear the patch."

Despite reminders that Vancouver Police Department officers are prohibited from wearing unauthorized patches, an officer was spotted with a thin blue line patch featuring an Israeli flag on his vest.

"You cannot put a price on public safety, and you cannot put a price on mental health and wellness," said ABC Vancouver Coun. Sarah Kirby-Yung, who is married to a VPD officer.

but apparently you can put a price on it
a $16 million top-up price

a breathstopping price

WORKPLACE SAFETY

We strive for the best results

Two VPD officers used police headquarters to shoot a video mocking internal sexual harassment investigations and shared it with their colleagues, according to a new report from BC's Office of the Police Complaint Commissioner (OPCC).

The 2019 video, which served to "ridicule and minimize" these probes, was spread to "numerous" officers, including a supervisor, who forwarded it on without taking any action.

Four unidentified officers were disciplined after an investigation was ordered by the commissioner.

One of BC's police watchdogs says it wants to go outside of the province to find an investigator into a series of allegations about what happened in a course that trains undercover police officers.

CTV News has learned that course, the BC Municipal Undercover Program, which was attended by the VPD and other BC law enforcement agencies, was shut down abruptly in May 2022 following allegations several officers went to extreme lengths in a course scenario to prove they are not a cop.

Those actions are alleged to include exposing genitalia, defecating on another officer, penetrating an officer using a vegetable, and removing feminine hygiene products, multiple sources confirmed to CTV News.

as a poet it is both believable and unbelievable to me
that the VPD has a poem about working dogs on their website
entitled "Guardians of the Night," author unknown
written in the first-person perspective of a dog

the poem is often read at memorial services for dogs killed on duty
and is composed of a service dog's declarations of submissive love
to her handler, for example, "When all others have left you
and the loneliness of the night closes in, I will be at your side"

there are policing and military versions of the poem, the latter of which
lands differently when the handler is a soldier in a combat zone
rather than a cop who gets to return to the safety of home every night

who knew attending to cop loneliness is a cop dog's job, not me
though I suspect the "others" who have left cops are spouses of cops
who have left their cop spouses because of domestic violence
a violence perpetrated more frequently by police than the public

as a creative writing instructor I might teach this poem
as a dramatic monologue, a poetic form written to sound like a speech
with a speaker addressing an intended auditor, and the speaker's
personality or character is shown to the reader through what they say,
that is, through what the writer makes the speaker say

in this case a cop dog is the speaker, a cop is the intended listener
and the cop-dog speaker's personality is shown through what she says
that is, through what the writer makes her say

for example, when the cop-dog speaker of the poem says
"It is for you that I will unselfishly give my life,
and spend my nights unrested," she is characterized as
willing to die rather than trained to die
for a "you" that is a cop, not the public

but dogs can't talk and that means no dogs have ever said to cops
the kinds of things this cop-dog speaker says to her handler
so the writer's characterization of the cop-dog speaker
actually reveals cop expectations of how cop dogs should be

cop dogs are trained to listen to their cop handler's commands
but I have questions about this stanza:

"I will quietly listen to you and pass no judgement,
nor will your spoken words be repeated.
I will remain ever silent, ever vigilant, and ever loyal."

what is the cop confessing to that ought not be repeated
and why does the author of the poem make the dog listen
"quietly" and promise to keep cop secrets

CBC News's research found that 158 of the more than 453
cop suspensions in Ontario from 2013 to 2024
involved gender-based violence
42.41 percent of the 158 suspensions are for domestic violence
44.3 percent of the 158 suspensions are for sexual assault

perhaps the secret the dog keeps is that the handler abuses his wife
which must be kept secret otherwise how will women who have been
abused by their partners be able to report domestic violence to the cops

perhaps the secret the dog keeps is that the handler is a sexual predator
like former VPD cop Jim Fisher of the VPD's Counter Exploitation Unit
who in 2018 was jailed for 20 months after pleading guilty to
2 counts of breach of trust 1 count of sexual exploitation
like former VPD cop Jagraj Roger Berar who was
convicted of sexual assault of a VPD officer in 2021
like like like like like like—

To Chief Constable Dave Jones, New Westminster PD

January 7, 2019

Impact Statement regarding Sgt. Dave Van Patten

This incident had changed who I am as a person. I was already suffering from mental health challenges and this incident aggravated my condition. I was betrayed, coerced, and taken advantage of by somebody who I respected and looked up to.

Since trying to go back to work in February 2018, I've developed a fear of being inside other people's homes. I feel unsafe and the constant need to escape, which I believe stems from what I maintain was a sexual assault inside Dave's apartment.

Before I was a solutions-based person and not someone who gives up easily. I joined the force when I was 19 years old. It was my dream to serve the public as a law enforcement officer. I left school early to be hired by the VPD as soon as possible.

If I brought this incident upon myself, I would be accountable for everything that happened. But I was sick and taken advantage of by a senior officer handling my file. There was a huge imbalance of power and I was severely depressed. I was honest with the department about my struggles and Dave used this information to exploit and manipulate me. I don't want this to ever happen to any of my colleagues. Through this process, I hope it's clear that Dave is not someone who should have the privilege of continuing as a police officer.

Please help me get some justice.

Sincerely,
Nicole Chan

Police Chief Palmer's Statement
on the Coroner's Inquest regarding the tragic death of Nicole Chan

February 1, 2023

Constable Nicole Chan chose a noble profession and devoted her
career to helping people in their time of need. That she died alone, of
suicide, and when she herself was in need, is something that will stay
with us always.

My heartfelt condolences to Nicole's family, her friends, and others
touched by her death.

Her life and career were tragically cut short, however. Nicole's death has
highlighted the importance of accountability in policing.

The Coroner's inquest into Nicole's death has been powerful, emotional,
and thought-provoking. It has deeply impacted us all.

Though we will take time to review the jury's recommendations, we
remain committed to

Nicole's death

According to the *Tyee,* on the recommendation of the VPD, Chan began seeing a psychologist in May 2016. On multiple occasions, the psychologist communicated with Van Patten about Chan's mental health treatment.

Chan's WorkSafeBC claim, approved in November 2018, alleges that Van Patten told Chan he had access to her human resources files and medical information and told Chan not to speak about their relationship.

In summer 2016, Van Patten discovered photos and messages on the phone of another officer who had had a sexual relationship with Chan. Van Patten videoed that material and threatened to tell Chan's and the other officer's spouses.

Under pressure from this threat, Chan continued to have sex with Van Patten. "I felt coerced into having sex and continuing the relationship."

In the WorkSafeBC claim, Chan also described a second sexual relationship, between her and another VPD superior, Sgt. Greg McCullough:

"I was of the belief that McCullough was the one person who understood what I was going through as he had experienced dealing with depression, had experienced suicidal thoughts, and I believed he had significant military training dealing with PTSD and depression. I thought I could trust him because of this and because he was my supervisor."

Chan's WorkSafeBC claim included an email from McCullough: "Nicole, I only wanted to help you get better. We became emotionally and then physically involved. I should have known better than to let this happen when what you needed most of all was a true friend."

According to a Canadian Press article reposted by *Blue Line*, Canada's law enforcement magazine, the Office of the Police Complaint Commissioner (OPCC) released its disciplinary decision, and Van Patten was dismissed from the force about a year after Chan's death. It came following a Police Act investigation that concluded four allegations of discreditable conduct against him were substantiated.

The OPCC found McCullough failed to disclose his relationship with Chan as well, according to an email obtained by CTV News. The then sergeant was given a 15-day suspension for "discreditable conduct," according to the OPCC, which said he had entered into a relationship with Chan "knowing that she was in a vulnerable state mentally and emotionally."

City of Vancouver Budget Expense Highlights:

The expenditure drivers and increases related to The City's current-state resources and service levels include significant increases in premiums resulting from increases in claim rates, particularly in the area of

workplace safety

safety does not look like

100 new cops

100 new Car 87 nurses

a Rururemoned finance bro mayor buddying up with a billionaire

cops investigating themselves

cops opting for retirement then joining the military

big trucks with thin blue line stickers gunning their motors

decamping the DTES

calling security on aunties and poh pohs practising tai chi
in Chinatown Plaza because they don't have a permit

Indigenous mothers writing their children's names
on their children's arms so the children can be identified
if their limbs become separated from their bodies
if their bodies are not intact

Indigenous mothers and families investigating
their daughters' disappearances and murders
because the police's negligent investigations
ascertain their daughters' deaths unsuspicious
even when their daughters' bodies are not intact

Gastown/Chinatown/Strathcona/Railtown residents who loved
Everything Everywhere All at Once but don't care about
displacing aunties and poh pohs who look like the protagonist

protection of property over poor people

corporate values of a Fun City with Swagger

determining a teenaged white boy's racist threats unthreatening

cops at the Memorial March, cops at Pride

momentarily worn orange shirts over VPD uniform for photo op

"see something say something"

a Vancouver branch of the Bank of Montreal's staff calling 911 on a
grandfather for trying to open a bank account for his granddaughter
using their government-issued Indian Status cards

the VPD handcuffing a grandfather, Maxwell Johnson of the Haíłzaqv
Nation, and his granddaughter, for being Indigenous while trying to open
a bank account

wellness checks

compassion fatigue and inattentional blindness

feminisms that seek to punish that essentialize

golf shirts and smaller guns

deploying detective sniffer dogs and
the recently rebranded Community-Industry Response Group
at protests calling for the end of the killing of children

people at CRAB park drinking $8 coffees saying unhoused people
shouldn't have the pets they have for companionship and safety while
the expensive-coffee drinkers' purebred dogs piss on the grass
people would like to sit on

weaponizing dogs

the VPD tweeting a donation request for easily militarized cybertrucks
at the billionaire who bought a social media platform to stop the "woke
mind virus" from infecting the platform

the fire marshal's order to decamp the DTES over fire concerns

a femme aflame on the street

failing to inform businesses located in a 100-year-old building
that said building is on fire watch

failing to inform residents living in a 100-year-old building
that said building is on fire watch

empty fire extinguishers at a 100-year-old building on fire watch

cop-enforced injunctions to dismantle tent cities

diverse hiring and cultural awareness training

blue walls of silence

any "team" whose name begins with "Assertive"

being incarcerated under the Mental Health Act

in her breathgiving book *Ordinary Notes*, Christina Sharpe says:

> Care is complicated, gendered, misused. It is often mobilized to enact violence, not assuage it, yet I cannot surrender it.
>
> I want acts and accounts of care as shared and distributed risk, as mass refusals of the unbearable life, as total rejection of the dead future.

I want that too

The City regularly realigns existing resources and spending levels in response to changes in demand for services and to

address risk

The 2023 Operating Budget includes $30.8 million of Council-directed investments in new initiatives that are required to fill service gaps, enhance service levels, and

address risk

Investment Highlights of the 2023 Operating Budget:

$21.9 million to support

   public safety

Initial funding to hire additional police officers to enhance and
expand mental health initiatives and partnerships between VPD and
Vancouver Coastal Health (VCH), such as the Car 87 program, Assertive
Community Treatment (ACT) teams, and Assertive Outreach Team
(AOT)

$5.5 million for community support

Address accessibility legislation and support outstanding work on

   safety

related to Missing and Murdered Indigenous Women and Girls

INDIGENOUS WOMEN, GIRLS, NONBINARY, AND TWO SPIRIT PEOPLES' SAFETY

Notes to Operating Budget table, con't.:

Arts, Culture, and Community Services – The 2023 Operating Budget reflects estimated increases (1) in fixed costs mainly in compensation and benefit expenses for existing resource levels, higher energy and building costs related to non-market housing, and lease and moving costs for 310 Main Street and DTES street market, (2) to address forthcoming accessibility legislation effective in 2023, and (3)

to complete outstanding work on

safety

related to Missing and Murdered Indigenous Women and Girls

In 2022, the deaths of three missing young Indigenous people, Chelsea Poorman, Noelle "Ellie" O'Soup, and Tatyanna Harrison, were confirmed. Their remains were discovered in different locations across the Lower Mainland within a 6-month time frame.

Chelsea   was reported missing September 8, 2020

Ellie   was reported missing May 12, 2021

Tatyanna   was reported missing May 3, 2022

Chelsea, Ellie, and Tatyanna's families say
the police delayed posting notices to the public
after reporting their loved ones missing

Chelsea's mother waited for 11 days

Ellie's auntie waited for 8 days

Tatyanna's mother waited for 9 days

Chelsea was so young, 24 years old

the VPD determined that Chelsea's death wasn't suspicious, though they haven't determined what the cause of her death was

Chelsea's mother said, "We're going to fight for Chelsea and we're going to fight for the truth and what happened to her."

how could Chelsea have gotten to the location where her body was found: Chelsea, who had a physical disability, was last seen in downtown Vancouver by her sister but was found in the backyard of a $7 million property in the wealthy neighbourhood of Shaughnessy, 6 kilometres away

how police could determine Chelsea's death unsuspicious given the condition in which her body was discovered

the day Chelsea's remains were discovered, April 22, 2022, was the last day Tatyanna was seen alive, but the police didn't notify Chelsea's mother that Chelsea's remains were found until two weeks later

as of August 15, 2023, the VPD have refused to release an external RCMP review that examined how the force investigated Chelsea's disappearance and death, saying that making the report public could compromise their ongoing investigation

Chelsea is loved, Chelsea is missed

Tatyanna was so young, 20 years old

Richmond RCMP determined that Tatyanna's death wasn't suspicious, as the coroner said the cause of death was "fentanyl toxicity," though the coroner's report, completed in February 2023, concluded that the cause of death was sepsis

Tatyanna's mother said, "On Aug. 8, I was informed of the circumstances her body was found in. This has brought more questions than police have answers."

how could Tatyanna have gotten to the location where her body was found: Tatyanna was living in the Downtown Eastside but was found in a dry-docked yacht at a Richmond marina 21 kilometres away, with no public transit nearby

how police could determine Tatyanna's death unsuspicious given the condition in which her body was discovered

it was Tatyanna's mother who found her missing daughter, not the VPD, as she connected reportage of an unidentified female body in Richmond to her daughter's disappearance

according to the coroner's report, "At one point, coroners' service investigators and police compared the missing person photo of Tatyanna Harrison with images taken of the woman found on the boat, but concluded they were not the same person"

Tatyanna is loved, Tatyanna is missed

Ellie was so young, 13 years old

Ellie's remains were found in an SRO room rented by Van Chung Pham, who repeatedly lured young women to his room to give them drugs

even though immigration authorities declared him a danger to the public in 2019 because a woman had died of an overdose in his former residence and because he sold fentanyl to vulnerable drug users, and in 2020, a young woman reported to the VPD that Pham gave her drugs then sexually assaulted her while she was incapacitated, it wasn't until May 2021, one day after Ellie went missing from a group home, that the VPD recommended charging Pham with sexual assault, overcoming resistance by administering a drug, and trafficking cocaine and heroin. When police arrived at the SRO on February 23, 2022 to arrest Pham, they found him dead

the VPD didn't find Ellie's remains, and the remains of another woman, in the 100-square-foot room, until more than two months later, on May 1

Ellie's family were lobbying the Ministry of Children and Family Development to have Ellie removed from the group home and placed in their care instead

Ellie is loved, Ellie is missed

CHINATOWN PUBLIC SAFETY

SAFETY

We strive for the best results

according to the VPD's Year-End 2020 Report:

"The most disturbing crime trend was the dramatic increase in anti-Asian hate crime and hate incidents. Sadly, hate crime incidents targeting the East Asian community increased by 717 percent in 2020."

are the sexual harassment and extortion Nicole Chan suffered
at the hands of white cops
an anti-Asian hate crime or
a gender-based hate crime or
an anti-Asian gender-based hate crime

as a Chinese Canadian, I question the Uplifting Chinatown Action Plan that is informed by City staff applying "observations and lessons" from the VPD's visit to San Francisco's Chinatown in August 2022. I question who the "community leaders" are that also participated in the trip and shared their findings at a Vancouver Police Board meeting.

are these "community leaders" the ones who rescinded intergenerational community group Chinatown Together and LGBTQ+ group Vancouver Lunar New Year For All's participation in the 2024 Lunar New Year parade?

teslas and towers with teeth multiply in the night
while Chinatown is eaten up by Michelin stars attempting to spit out
youth and elders who fight against
business improvement areas and gentrification

but The City of Vancouver is no match
for auntie and poh poh resistance
aunties and poh pohs made nimble
by Mrs. Ma's tai chi practice

the Uplifting Chinatown Action Plan has a three-pillar approach:

cleaning and sanitation
graffiti removal and placemaking
community supports

$1,340,000 for cleaning and sanitation

people say they're tired of how much shit is on the sidewalks and I get it, I don't want to see or smell shit, but we all shit, and we all deserve the dignity of being able to shit in a sanitary space

there is $280,000 for desperately needed "increased access to public washrooms" but there is also $750,000 for "feces collection" which could be used to build low-income housing and public washrooms so people wouldn't have to shit on the street

$660,000 for graffiti removal and placemaking

what placemaking will happen for low-income Chinese seniors?

$50,000 for community supports

why are "community supports" allotted the lowest amount in the Uplifting Chinatown Property Values Action Plan, why is it going to the Vancouver Chinatown Business Improvement Area Society?

July 1, 2023, is the centennial of the Chinese Exclusion Act, which was passed on the day some people celebrate Canada's natal occasion but was called Humiliation Day by some Chinese Canadians

on July 1, the Chinese Canadian Museum opened in the historic Wing Sang Building, Chinatown's oldest building, which was previously owned by art collector and real estate marketer Bob Rennie

the opening exhibition, *The Paper Trail to the 1923 Chinese Exclusion Act*, was welcomed by delegates, including Mayor Sim, The City's first mayor of Chinese ethnicity

"The Chinese Canadian Museum will serve as a testament to the endurance, the triumphs, and the immeasurable contributions of Chinese Canadians to our city and our country," said Sim.

as a Chinese Canadian, I take no pride in
Vancouver's first Chinese Canadian mayor
no pride in the exclusion of low-income Chinese seniors
resulting from gentrification in Chinatown and the DTES

as a Chinese Canadian, I take pride in
the youth of the Yarrow Intergenerational Society for Justice

who ameliorate language and cultural barriers Chinatown and
DTES seniors face // who provide help with transportation and
accompaniment to medical appointments // who deliver culturally
appropriate groceries // who organize cultural events // who offer
harm-reduction workshops // who provided pivotal care for Chinese
seniors during the pandemic, which is still ongoing, a pandemic which
saw a steep rise in anti-Asian hate crimes // who oppose the 105 Keefer
development

as a Chinese Canadian, I'll always remember when Jenny Kwan

who in 1993 was elected as the youngest Vancouver city councillor,
spoke Cantonese in televised council meetings so her constituents
could understand her, despite the anti-Asian racism she experienced for
doing so

as a Chinese Canadian, I take pride in Chinatown Together

who successfully fought the 2024 Chinatown Spring Festival
Celebration Committee's rejection of their application to march in the
New Year parade // who successfully fought the committee again, when
it rescinded the group's invitation because of their "political activism,"
and marched in the parade // who takes on The City's new Chinatown
zoning policies, arguing for a public hearing process, pointing out
how the bid for Chinatown to be designated a World Heritage Site
will be negatively impacted by culturally inappropriate real estate
developments like 105 Keefer

care looks like

100,000 new social housing units

1,000 new public washrooms

catching people when they're trying to defy gravity

using the buddy system to and from a blockade
that shut down The City's port, the biggest port in Canada
third-largest port in North America

providing fire extinguishers to unhoused people
who use fire to keep warm and to cook food

food security and access to clean water

Masks4EastVan

OPS vans and naloxone training and safe supply

looking away if a hungry person takes food they didn't pay for

fighting for social housing and affordable housing

fighting for an inclusive equitable Chinatown

a radical rethinking of rights
that moves from individualism and charity to mutual aid

a living wage and free transit

feeding the hungry children of Vancouver
who need food programs at their schools not cops

shared risk

understanding fight/flight/freeze/fawn trauma responses

peer-to-peer support, VANDU, WAHRS

your workmates grabbing extra bad date sheets, condoms,
and lube in case you missed the van

Tracey Morrison walking towards you
bannock in one hand, clean syringes in the other

hundreds and thousands in the streets
despite police surveillance and violence

care pods and chosen families

assistive technologies like vibrating or flashing-light alert systems to
warn Deaf residents of fire in their 100-year-old building on fire watch

a 5-hour Palestinian poetry sit-in led by students
despite those students already being positioned as
a threat to student safety

a fully funded Canada Disability Benefit

Crips for eSims for Gaza

a daughter and father staging a model minority mutiny

consent-based models of medical treatment

defunding disarming dismantling

then rebuilding from the ground up

Muriel and Su and the dogs
murmurate up the Pacific coastline
travel pattern learned from starling kin
deployed to avoid being tracked

taking the inland freeway back is quicker
but they know how much the dogs need to play
to play with each other
play in the sand breathe in the salted air
run without command run with each other
piss on their own schedule smell each other's butts
track no scent other than their own
their scent changing the further they get from
being weapons

the pack grows as Su and Muriel move north
Spot carries the dogs whose knees are damaged from the job
when they get to the Canadian–American border
the dogs run up over under around the vehicles waiting to cross
a black-and-tan wave of fur undulating liberation in every direction

the border cops observe but are too busy
trying to gain control over their canine subordinates
who are running to join the pack

Su and Muriel and the dogs
bust open the VPD canine training facility, free the dogs
go to Winnipeg, to the only police force in Canada to have
a robot dog — so far — and release this Spot too

taking up the VPD motto, Servamus, "We Protect"
the pack disperses themselves: some form poh poh protection squads,
several congregate in Chinatown and the DTES to keep unhoused
people and low-income people safe, they keep 6 on the SLOs in
Vancouver high schools, they keep Nicole's family safe from harm, they
keep Jay's family safe from harm, they keep Chelsea's family safe from
harm, they keep Tatyanna's family safe from harm, they keep Ellie's
family safe from harm, they go any and everywhere people need to be
kept safe from the police

ACKNOWLEDGMENTS

To the families of Chelsea Poorman, Tatyanna Harrison, and Noelle O'Soup, I hope this book honours your loved ones.

I sought but did not receive permission from the families of Chelsea Poorman, Tatyanna Harrison, and Noelle "Ellie" O'Soup to write about their loved ones. I attempted contact several times through various means, anxiously negotiating the line between diligence in seeking permissions and pestering. As time passed and I didn't hear back, I struggled with how to proceed. Given my intention to honour Chelsea, Tatyanna, and Ellie's lives and to hold the police accountable for failing to protect them, could I go forward without permissions? Is that disrespectful regardless of intentions? What about the capacities of the families, who are mourning, to respond to a stranger's non-journalistic inquiry about their children's deaths. Is a lack of response a "no"? It is not a "yes."

Ultimately, I decided to include the poems about Chelsea, Tatyanna, and Ellie. An accurate critique of the VPD must address their refusal to keep Indigenous women, girls, nonbinary, and Two Spirit peoples safe from harm. To omit the VPD's negligence in handling the disappearances and deaths of Chelsea, Tatyanna, and Ellie would mean I would be negligent in my duty of care to communities I am accountable to. To exclude them feels unethical to me, an act of violence through erasure. I will remain accountable as this book enters the public sphere.

Thank you Laura Holland for permission to write about your son, Jared "Jay" Lowndes. I hope this book honours him.

To Nicole Chan's family, I hope this book honours Nicole.

Thank you Lorelei Williams and Jen St. Denis for relaying communications, for your advocacy, and for all your work in community.

Thanks to the Talonbooks team, especially Ryan Fitzpatrick for your assiduous eye and Catriona Strang for texting me anti-Sim posters.

Thank you Magín Manolete and Meenakshi Mannoe of Defund 604 Network and Justice for Jared for your anti-cop reportage, actions, and art.

Love and gratitude to Bev Ho, Billy-Ray Belcourt, the bridge builders on the Territories of the Anishinaabeg and Haudenosaunee Peoples, Cassandra Blanchard, Chinatown Together, Cynthia Dewi-Oka, Dallas Hunt, David Chariandy, Fred Moten, Hari Alluri, Harjap Grewal, Harsha Walia, Jacqueline Turner, Jen Currin, Junie Désil, Karen Ward, Keimi Nakashima-Ochoa, Melody Ma, Muriel Marjorie, Nyki Kish, Phanuel Antwi, Sheung Leung, Yarrow Intergenerational Society for Justice, and my sweetie and our house panthers. Extra love and gratitude to Rita Wong. Extra extra love and gratitude to Cecily Nicholson.

NOTES

In response to scholar Christina Sharpe's question "Can an account of care have an analysis of power?" *cop city swagger* takes a deep dive into the words "safety" and "care," conducting an inquiry into whose safety matters in the City of Vancouver. Engaging a documentary methodology, I searched for evidence of the VPD's and The City's acts of harms from publicly available sources such as The City of Vancouver's current budget; the VPD's website, press releases, and official reports; the BC Community Alliance Group's open letter regarding the VSB and VPD's response to a racist hate crime at a Vancouver high school; a press release from BC's Office of the Human Rights Commissioner critiquing the use of School Liaison Officers in schools; the ABC-controlled VBS's proposed motion to reinstate of the School Liaison Officer program; and local and national news. I assess the Vancouver Police Department; the business practices of Vancouver's first Chinese Canadian mayor, the first Vancouver mayor publicly endorsed by the Vancouver Police Union; and The City's current budget. Campaigning on the promise to address safety by increasing the number of cops on the streets, the mayor, Ken Sim, swaggered into office and began to run The City like a business. Evidenced by the VPD's acts of violence against women, Black and Indigenous People and People of Colour, people with mental illnesses, and people who are unhoused and low-income, my threat assessment shows that the police are dangerous and their version of safety means harm.

Alice Walker wrote "Those who love us never leave us alone with our grief. At the moment they show us our wound, they reveal they have the medicine." After showing the wounds caused by the VPD and mayor, I hope my foregrounding of collective acts of care as alternatives to policing provide some medicine. I hope the threads of community resistance to the police sewn throughout *cop city swagger*, as well as the dreams/plans/actions towards an inclusive and culturally vibrant Chinatown, provide some medicine.

I've been needing some medicine, as it's been difficult and triggering to finish writing this book that condemns the VPD when serial killer Robert Pickton is in the news again. I was a sex worker in the Downtown Eastside in the 1990s when Pickton was active and witnessed first-hand the VPD's egregious negligence in investigating the disappearances and murders of women from the area, many of whom were Indigenous. When I started writing this book, research often led me to the Pickton case but I ignored these search results. I'd already written a book about it, and needed to protect myself from the grisly forensic details of Canada's largest crime scene to date that so titillated the public. Nevertheless, intrusive images of corpses began to haunt me. In February 2024, he became eligible for day parole, and while it was unlikely it would be granted, I was still surprised and upset by the news.

In March, a comedy trio whose act includes joke about residential schools and mass graves, made a gruesome, disturbing T-shirt to sell on their upcoming tour that featured an image of Pickton holding a strip of bacon and the tagline, "Over 50 Flavours of Hookery Smoked Bacon." Sisters Sage's Instagram page reported that the trio's dehumanizion of the women whose disappearances and murders were ignored by the VPD and RCMP "was met with fire from the Indigenous community across so called Canada, and their idiotic shows have been cancelled in other cities." Lynn-Marie and Melissa-Rae Angus created Sisters Sage, a business that sells handmade self-care products informed by the sisters' Indigenous cultural traditions and is all about community resistance, consciousness raising, and mutual aid from Vancouver to Gaza.

The Vancouver show was cancelled, but the trio found a venue willing to platform comedians who joke about genocide, a venue they kept secret for "their safety," alleging they had received death threats. Butterflies in Spirit, a group of Indigenous performers who dance to raise awareness of violence against Indigenous women and girls, organized a rally against the comedians, location TBA. Started in 2012 by Palexelsiya Lorelei Williams, Butterflies in Spirit are family members of Missing and Murdered Indigenous Women. They often dance in T-shirts that feature their loved ones' images and have performed locally, nationally, and internationally to wide critical acclaim.

It turns out that the undisclosed venue was a gym in Chinatown, just a few blocks from the Downtown Eastside, Pickton's hunting ground. The night of the show, VPD officers stood guard at the entrance. Why? To protect the comedians from family and community members protesting the show? I felt crazy seeing the VPD serve as private security to protect comedians who make jokes about the women the VPD failed to protect. But I didn't feel surprised. Because the VPD hasn't changed at all since Pickton.

In May 2024, Pickton was attacked, then died two weeks later. In a way his death is a relief. But the fact that Indigenous women, girls and Two Spirit people are killed at a rate 12 times higher than non-Indigenous women is a systemic problem, not a problem perpetrated solely by an individual. After Pickton's trial, after the 2012 Provincial Inquiry, after the 2016 National Inquiry, after the 2019 publication of *Reclaiming Power and Place: The Final Report of the National Inquiry Into Missing and Murdered Indigenous Women and Girls* and the *Executive Summary of the Final Report*, which begins with a definition of genocide – the VPD continues to disregard the safety of Indigenous women and children.

What has changed enormously is the public's awareness of Missing and Murdered Indigenous Women, Girls, Nonbinary, and Two Spirit People, due to the fortitude and the concerted, sustained efforts of Indigenous people, families, and communities who fight for justice for their beloveds.

SOURCES

Over the course of the book, I quote faithfully and unfaithfully from a number of police, government, and news media sources. I sometimes retain errors, in particular typos, from the original sources.

The epigraphs are from K-Ming Chang's *Gods of Want* (2022), and from Christina Sharpe, as moderator of a plenary panel at Care and Cure, the York University Strategies of Containment conference (2023).

Both the City of Vancouver's "Mission and Values" statement and the *Vancouver 2023 Budget* report are texts that this book returns to again and again.

"xʷməθkʷəy̓əm Nation's Values" cites the xʷməθkʷəy̓əm/Musqueam Nation's web page on "Mission, Vision, Values"; the Sḵwx̱wú7mesh/ Squamish Nation's 2026 Strategic Plan; *CBC News'* June 16, 2018, article "Paddle Song Performed to Thank Indigenous Responders to Great Vancouver Fire"; the səlilwətaɬ/Tsleil Waututh Nation's 2022– 2025 Strategic Plan; the City of Vancouver's web page "Mission and Values"; and the VPD's web page "About the VPD: Beyond the Call." I took the photograph in Chinatown on August 18, 2023.

"A Better City is now ABC Vancouver!" draws from an April 2022 press release announcing ABC Vancouver and Ken Sim's electoral campaign.

"ABC Vancouver to expand Car 87/88 program" draws from an August 2022 election press release.

"safe (adjective)" draws from three sources: the *Oxford English Dictionary* definition for "safe"; the *Wikipedia* web page on "safety"; and the *Online Etymology Dictionary* definitions of "safe" and "safety."

"I envision a Vancouver in the not-so-distant" draws from Dan Fumano's January 25, 2023, *Vancouver Sun* column "Mayor Ken Sim Aims to Make Vancouver 'Swagger' Again – What Does That Mean?"

"Q: The public knows" draws from an October 21, 2022, *Vancouver Sun* interview with Ken Sim conducted by Lori Culbert titled "Vancouver Mayor-Elect Ken Sim Talks Racism, Heavy Metal Music, and Losing Friends to Drugs."

"According to the *Times Colonist*" draws from two sources: Rumneek Johal's October 7, 2022, *Press Progress* article "Vancouver Mayoral Candidate Ken Sim Co-Owned a Long-Term Care Staffing Firm That Was Mired in Controversy"; and Russ Francis's February 25, 2005, *Tyee* article "Seniors Suffer from Contracting Out."

"A July 27 inspection report" also draws from Francis's 2005 *Tyee* article.

"Q: Have you maintained a connection with your working-class roots" draws from Culbert's 2022 interview with Ken Sim.

"Vancouver Police Chief Adam Palmer was called to respond" draws from Andrew Weichel's April 27, 2022, *CTV News* article "Vancouver Police Not Using Thin Blue Line Patches as White Supremacist Symbol, Chief Says."

"Vancouver police have apologized" draws from three sources: Simon Little's May 14, 2021, *Global News* article "Vancouver Police Mistakenly Handcuff Retired BC Supreme Court Judge"; UBC's Peter A. Allard School of Law History Project's online profile "The Honourable Selwyn Romilly;" and Alexander Vaz's September 27, 2023, *Chilliwack Progress* article "Selwyn Romilly, B.C.'s First Black Judge, Dies at Age 83."

"Police Chief's Statement on the tragic death of Tyre Nichols" draws from a January 28, 2023, VPD press release titled "Statement from Chief Adam Palmer on the Tragic Death of Tyre Nichols."

"Ken Sim reflects on his first 100 days as mayor" draws from Justin McElroy's February 15, 2023, *CBC News* article "'A Positive Vibe': 100 Days In, Vancouver's Mayor Talks about the Goals of SimCity."

"City claims 'staff error' caused four traffic cameras to go offline" draws from Elana Shepert's April 5, 2023, *Vancouver is Awesome* article "City Claims 'Staff Error Caused 4 Traffic Cameras to Go Offline as It Moved Out DTES Campers."

"City crews continue to clear tents and encampments" draws from Amy Judd and Kristen Robinson's April 11, 2023, *Global News* article "'We're Happy with the Progress That's Made': Vancouver Mayor on Hastings Street Decampment."

"Internal emails at Vancouver Shitty Hall" draws from Nathan Griffiths's June 4, 2023, *Vancouver Sun* article "What Internal City of Vancouver Records Reveal about Removing the DTES Camp."

"Section 7 of the Canadian Charter of Rights and Freedoms recognizes" draws from Dexter McMillan's June 27, 2019, *Tyee* article "The Charter of Rights Can Protect Homeless Campers. Is That Enough?"

"The decision to remove the Hastings Street camp comes despite" draws from Bridgette Watson's April 5, 2023, *CBC News* article "Vancouver Police, City Staff Begin Removing Encampment on East Hastings Street."

"According to *CBC News*, members of the Vancouver Police Department have been reminded" draws from Bethany Lindsay's January 19, 2023, *CBC News* article "Vancouver Police Confirm Thin Blue Line Patch Isn't Allowed on Officer's Uniforms."

"Despite reminders that Vancouver Police Department officers are prohibited" draws from Defund 604's April 5, 2023, post on X, which you can view on X or in Elana Shepert's April 10, 2023, *Vancouver is Awe-*

some article "Vancouver Police Officer Spotted Wearing Unauthorized 'Thin Blue Line' Patch During Encampment."

"Muriel and Su learn about Jared Lowndes from the eagles" draws from three sources: the *Justice for Jared* website; Amanda Follett Hosgood's December 2, 2022, *Tyee* article "Police Watchdog Recommends Charges for Shooting Death of Jared Lowndes"; and the July 7, 2023, *Global News* article "'Unaccountable Systems': Wet'suwet'en Man's Family Sues B.C. RCMP over Shooting Death." It takes its final quote from the Independent Investigations Office of BC's October 27, 2023, press release "IIO Has Submitted Report to Crown Counsel for Consideration of Charges Regarding the Death of One Man in Campbell River in July 2021 (2021-179)."

"Su and Muriel can't imagine the anger and frustration" quotes from the RCMP's web page on "Police dogs" and draws elements from the VPD's web page on "VPD Police Service Dogs."

"ABC-Vancouver commits to restoring honours programs" draws from four sources: a September 2022 election press release; an "advisor insight" post from the *rennie* website on "Top Public Secondary Schools in Vancouver"; the Vancouver School Board's School History web pages on Magee and Eric Hamber Secondary Schools; and the December 23, 2023, *Griffin's Nest* article "Nine New Year's Resolutions for the VSB."

"In 2018, Changich Baboth, a Black student at Vancouver's Lord Byng Secondary School" draws from two *Tyee* articles by Katie Hyslop: the September 11, 2019, article "How a Black Student Paid the Price for Racism at a Vancouver School"; and the November 20, 2020, article "Two Years Ago, a Racist Video Rocked a Vancouver School. Here's What Happened Since."

"August 27, 2019" draws from an open letter by the BC Community Alliance addressed to a number of VPD, City, provincial, and school representatives about the racist video a Lord Byng Secondary School student made.

"February 2, 2021" is an auto-fill letter template written by Cops Out of Schools for their first call to action for Black History Month, a weekend email buzz to VBS Trustees.

"Argyle is an international team" draws from Argyle PR's website.

"FOR IMMEDIATE RELEASE" draws from a November 25, 2022, press release from BC's Office of the Human Rights Commissioner titled "Letter to School Trustees on Human Rights Concerns with the Use of School Liaison Officers in BC schools."

"Changich Baboth, a Grade 12 student in the district" and "All I wanted in that moment was to be understood" both draw from Katie Hyslop's March 10, 2021, *Tyee* article "The Deep Divide on Police in Vancouver Schools Continues."

"New School Liaison Officer Program!" draws from Kevin Charach's April 20, 2023, *CTV News* article "Golf Shirts, Smaller Guns Part of VPD's 'Softening' Approach to Revamped School Liaison Officer Program."

"Outside of a Bronx elementary school" draws from Eric Lach's January 8, 2022, *New Yorker* article "Eric Adams Says He Has Swagger. What Else Does He Have?"

"Muriel and Su head south down the I-5" quotes from both the Los Angeles Police Foundation's and the Vancouver Police Foundation's "About Us" web pages, and draws from Linh Tat's May 23, 2023, *Los Angeles Daily News* article "LA City Council Approves a Robot Dog Named 'Spot' Donated to LAPD."

"The City's 2023 budget requires balancing" draws from Lisa Steacy's March 14, 2024, *CTV News* article "Here's How Many Times Vancouver's Mayor Has Been Absent from a Vote at Council" and Tori Marlan's February 14, 2024, *Investigative Journalism Foundation* article "Vancouver Mayor Ken Sim Votes to Send City Money to a Health Authority that Awards Millions in Contracts to His Private Home Care Company."

"Vancouver City Coun. Brian Montague" draws from Rafferty Baker's December 19, 2022, *CBC News* article "Vancouver City Councillor Defends Wearing Controversial Thin Blue Line Police Patch."

"Despite reminders that Vancouver Police Department officers" draws from Sean Orr's February 15, 2024, post on X, which you can view on X or in Isabella Zavarise's February 16, 2024, *CTV News* article "'It's Inflammatory': Vancouver Police Officer's Patch Ignites Questions about Objectivity."

"You cannot put a price on public safety" draws from Mike Howell's November 22, 2022, *Vancouver is Awesome* article "Vancouver Council Approves $16 Million for 100 Cops, 100 Nurses."

"Two VPD officers used police headquarters to shoot a video" draws from Bethany Lindsay's November 23, 2022, *CBC News* article "Vancouver Police Officers Mocked Internal Sexual Harassment Probes in Widely Shared Video, Report Shows."

"One of BC's police watchdogs says it wants to go outside" draws from Jon Woodward's May 31, 2022, *CTV News* article "'That Sounds Disgusting': Disturbing Allegations at BC Undercover Police Training Course."

"as a poet it is both believable and unbelievable" draws from six sources: the anonymously authored poem "Guardians of the Night" on the VPD's web page on "VPD Police Service Dogs"; Julie Ireton's April 24, 2024, *CBC News* article "'Blue Wall of Silence' Protects Police Officers Accused of Gender-Based Violence, Victims Say"; the British Columbia Prosecution Service's February 9, 2020, media statement "Special Prosecutor Releases Clear Statement" (on the appointment of a special prosecutor for the investigation into the conduct of VPD officers in relation to their investigation of former VPD detective James Fisher); Catherine Urquhart's February 7, 2024 *Global News* article "New Allegations Raised in Civil Suit Against Disgraced VPD Detective"; Catherine Urquhart's February 24, 2023 *Global News* article "Vancouver Police Officer Suing Former Colleague Convicted of Sexually Assaulting Her"; and Susan Lazaruk's October 13, 2023, *Vancouver Sun* article "BC: Six Female Police Officers Allege On-the-Job Sexual Harassment."

"To Chief Constable Dave Jones, New Westminster PD" quotes from Nicole Chan's January 7, 2019, "Impact Statement regarding Sgt. Dave Van Patten." I edited Nicole's statement for length — but no words, sentence structure and order, or paragraph order were changed.

"Police Chief Palmer's Statement" draws from the VPD's February 1, 2023, press release "Statement from Chief Constable Adam Palmer on Coroner's Inquest Verdict."

"According to the *Tyee*, on the recommendation of the VPD, Chan began seeing a psychologist" draws from Jen St. Denis and Katie Hyslop's February 9, 2023, *Tyee* article "A Tragic End to Nicole Chan's Fight for Justice in the VPD."

"In the WorkSafeBC claim, Chan also described" draws from Karin Larsen's January 25, 2023, *CBC News* article "Sexual Coercion by VPD Supervisor Alleged in Claim Made by Const. Nicole Chan Before She Died."

"According to a *Canadian Press* article reposted by *Blue Line*" draws from two sources: the *Blue Line* article which is a repost of *The Canadian Press*'s article; and Lisa Steacy's June 25, 2022, *CTV News* article "Family of Officer Who Died by Suicide Suing Vancouver Police Department, Former Sergeants."

"City of Vancouver Budget Expense Highlights:" draws from a 2023 City of Vancouver amended draft budget document.

"safety does not look like" draws from three sources: Michelle Gomez's June 27, 2023 *CBC News* article "City of Vancouver Apologizes for Kicking Low-Income Seniors out of Chinatown Mall During Tai Chi Meetup"; Angela Sterritt's January 9, 2020, *CBC News* article "Indigenous Grandfather and 12-Year-Old Handcuffed in front of Vancouver Bank after Trying to Open an Account"; and Amanda Follett Hosgood's February 2, 2024, *Tyee* article "The RCMP Sent Its Pipeline Protest Unit to Pro-Palestinian Rallies."

"In 2022, the deaths of three missing young Indigenous people" draws from Jen St. Denis's February 13, 2023, *Tyee* article "Chelsea, Noelle, and Tatyanna Went Missing. Did Police Do Enough to Find Them?"

"Chelsea was so young, 24 years old" draws from three sources: Michelle Ghoussoub's May 12, 2022, *CBC News* article "Chelsea Poorman's Body Lay in Shaughnessy for More Than a Year. But Her Death Was Not Considered Suspicious"; Jen St. Denis's May 9, 2022, *Tyee* article "What Happened to Chelsea?"; and Jen St. Denis's August 15, 2023, *Tyee* article "The VPD Won't Release a Review of Its Chelsea Poorman Investigation."

"Tatyanna was so young, 20 years old" draws from three sources: Michelle Ghoussoub's May 10, 2023, *CBC News* article "B.C. Coroner Concluded Tatyanna Harrison Died of Sepsis — Months After Police Said Fentanyl Was the Cause"; Jen St. Denis's February 13, 2023, *Tyee* article "Chelsea, Noelle, and Tatyanna Went Missing. Did Police Do Enough to Find Them?"; and the VPD's August 6, 2022, news release "Remains of missing Indigenous woman identified."

"Ellie was so young, 13 years old" draws from four sources: Jason Proctor, Michelle Ghoussoub, and Ethan Sawyer's October 3, 2022, *CBC News* article "Man Linked to Death of Noelle O'Soup Was Deemed 'Danger to Public' — Then Released from Immigration Custody"; Jason Proctor and Michelle Ghoussoub's January 24, 2023, *CBC News* article "Woman Describes in Warrant How Serial Offender Lured Her to Suite Where Noelle O'Soup Was Later Found Dead"; Jen St. Denis's February 13, 2023, *Tyee* article; and Jen St. Denis's August 24, 2022, *Tyee* article "'He Was Always with Other Girls Giving Them Free Drugs."

"according to the VPD's Year-End 2020 Report" draws from the VPD's "Vancouver Police Department 2020 Year in Review" report.

"as a Chinese Canadian" draws from Yasmin Gandham's March 9, 2024, *CTV News* article "Reclaiming Our Space: Chinatown Seniors Return to Mall to Practice Tai Chi."

"the Uplifting Chinatown Action Plan has a three-pillar approach" draws from a City of Vancouver Council Report from January 6, 2023, regarding the Uplifting Chinatown Action Plan.

"July 1, 2023, is the centennial of the Chinese Exclusion act" draws from Graeme Wood's June 30, 2023, *Vancouver is Awesome* article "Chinese Canadian Museum Set to Open on 100th Anniversary of Exclusion Act."

The devasting statistic comparing murder rates of women in Canada included in my notes is drawn from *Reclaiming Power and Place: The Final Report of the National Inquiry into Missing and Murdered Indigenous Women and Girls.*

Mercedes Eng is the author of *Mercenary English, Prison Industrial Complex Explodes*, winner of the Dorothy Livesay Poetry Prize, and *my yt mama*. Her writing has appeared in *Hustling Verse: An Anthology of Sex Workers' Poetry, Jacket 2, Asian American Literary Review, The Capilano Review*, and *The Abolitionist*. She was the Writer-in-Residence and a Shadbolt Fellow at Simon Fraser University, and recently co-curated her first exhibition with Keimi Nakashima-Ochoa, *Inside/Out: the art show my dad never had*. Mercedes teaches at Emily Carr University of Art + Design where she organizes the On Edge reading series.